PRAISE FOR *BLACK CALCULUS*

Norm Mattox's poems are full of empathy
hopefulness, longing, deep feeling, and son
ful poem by Pablo Neruda "The Chair," Mattox's poems resonate with history, the oft-felt but seldom voiced, the love-filled and the ineluctable. When I read his work, I want to play the saxophone. And if this is a musician's book, it is also—and powerfully—a griot's praise song.

KENNETH A. MCCLANE
W.E.B. Du Bois Professor of Literature Emeritus, Cornell University

Norm Mattox writes elegant poem/equations with answers we need for the deep corrections.
'stories change lives
the village narratives
integrate the world'
Mattox is a master poem architect. I encourage you to settle in for a while, in the stunning spaces he creates.

KIM SHUCK
7th Poet Laureate of San Francisco

Black Calculus is indeed the fabrics of space singing to you. And you can find Mr. Mattox, in a poem, picking tea leaves from the cities' jungle floors, returning with lyrics of fate. He must have written these poems for a bandstand. He must have raised himself in a saxophone case.

TONGO EISEN-MARTIN
author of *Heaven Is All Goodbyes* and *someone's dead already*

Black Calculus

Norm Mattox

NOMADIC PRESS

OAKLAND

111 FAIRMOUNT AVENUE
OAKLAND, CA 94611

BROOKLYN

475 KENT AVENUE #302
BROOKLYN, NY 11249

WWW.NOMADICPRESS.ORG

MISSION STATEMENT

Nomadic Press is a 501 (C)(3) not-for-profit organization that supports the works of emerging and established writers and artists. Through publications (including translations) and performances, Nomadic Press aims to build community among artists and across disciplines.

SUBMISSIONS

Nomadic Press wholeheartedly accepts unsolicited book manuscripts. To submit your work, please visit www.nomadicpress.org/submissions

DISTRIBUTION

Orders by trade bookstores and wholesalers:
Small Press Distribution,
1341 Seventh Street
Berkeley, CA 94701
spd@spdbooks.org
(510) 524-1668 / (800) 869-7553

Black Calculus

This book was made possible by a loving community of chosen family and friends, old and new.

For author questions or to book a reading at your bookstore, university/school, or alternative establishment, please send an email to info@nomadicpress.org.

Cover artwork and author portrait by Arthur Johnstone

Published by Nomadic Press, 111 Fairmount Avenue, Oakland, CA 94611

First printing, 2021

LIBRARY OF CONGRESS CATALOGING-IN-PUBLICATION DATA

Norm Mattox 1956 –
Title: *Black Calculus*
P. CM.
Summary: *Black Calculus* is about the essence of what connects us to each other, as well as to the living environment that surrounds us. This collection focuses on the love that is devoted to the dream of justice for all and the mandate to love one another.

[1. POETRY. 2. BLACK. 3. AMERICAN GENERAL.] I. III. TITLE.

LIBRARY OF CONGRESS CONTROL NUMBER: 2021932306

ISBN: 978-1-7363963-0-8

Black Calculus

Norm Mattox

NOMADIC
PRESS

CONTENTS

INTRODUCTION

Love is the common thread woven through each piece. Some of the poems "speak" the voice of admiration, adoration, and respect without using the word "love." Through poetry, I reflect on my feelings of joy, inspiration, tremendous frustration, of the enormous gratitude for the challenge of writing about love during these times. I am inspired to write about emotions connected to images and images connected to words and that connects with all the witnesses to that moment. I am changed by the words I am writing. My hope is that my poetry will change something in the reader, as well. This collection is about the essence that connects each one of us to everything else.

IN THE SHADOW OF ME

it will appear   that i am standing on a pedestal,   i'm actually a
mountain of shoulders   surrounded by a village of my ancestors
each one with a microphone   connected to the speaker.   my lips
moving the only sound   the echo feedback loop   creating a
chorus of   voices reciting my life like a mantra

a halo larger than the object   blocking the light.   sea foam
atomized by waves   crashing against themselves.   edges
made of smoke   deforming shapes fixed in memory,   a vision of their
greatest fear,   "they thought they saw..."

all they see is shade   hiding behind a mirage.   they thought
i had a gun   reaching for a loaded comb   to blow my brains out.
they asked for ID   hoping that i reach for it   so they
can be afraid for their lives.

        a silhouette of every Black man   fitting the description
that has been stopped,
                        frisked,
                                questioned and
                                                murdered
by accident   a perforated surface   mistaken for pores
        actual bullet holes   too many to count

an ecosystem beyond mind   where i can pay attention
to an infrared image   doesn't see both feet on fire
burning up my legs   while standing in this hell

the churn of tectonic plates   sliding underneath my skin
causing a flooded chest cavity   drowning between broken rib mountains
        assembled along rippling deltoids

holding guard over thundering pectorals

a shape with edges showing stretch marks
between an expanding dream filling with potent promise,
and a vessel deflating like a balloon with heaven escaping
through multiple gunshot wounds

a vision of hope shredded beyond recognition
another martyr recycled into the ancestor bin a soup of tears
mixed with bones and ashes simmered in hope over
a low flame for generations

chunks of soul boiled in molasses and bitter herbs
over time a sancocho of rock soup, a mainstay on the menu
served as chef's delight with an unearthly sazón

light burning through all substance not as dense
as the thought of a Black man absorbing the hate
shining resilience and the persistent glare of eyes on the prize
of an equitable struggle for us against unjust
decaying infrastructures of
systemic racism

an uprooted life returning to "roots"
nourished by gaiamundo calibrating the river channel's flow
to feed my tree of life all the xylem and phloem
my branches require
to sustain a full canopy

AT THE BEACH

i go to the beach
on days like this
to find my father.

any day i want to share
my water with the ocean

the sight of waves
falling over each other
scrambling to the shore,
conjures daddy watching
these very waves
as a seaman in the navy.
how many waves
rolled up on the shore
daddy's standing on,
right now?

the spectacle of kites
flying through multiple shades of wind,
retells
daddy's tales of kite flying
from Bronx tenement rooftops,
competing like fighting birds
with razor blades
in their embellished tails
cutting the cord
of an enemy kite
leaving it limp
falling
out of grace

hanging lame in the telephone
wires

standing on the beach
sands of time,
shifting,
falling
carrying the vibration signature
daddy's footsteps on Bermuda pink sands,
mostly Jones' Beach sometimes Zach's Bay the favorites
picking up impressions
humming like a voice in my ear.

a waning gibbous moon
reaching for the horizon,
meant time for blankets
to spread out on cool sands,
before ice melted
sandwiches wilted
grapes turned to plump raisins
wondering what a moon was doing
dancing in a morning sky.

breathing the same air recycled over decades
of consumption and re-creation. the idea of
daddy's last breath mixing with the new air
blowing off the ocean
carries the
iota
and the fullness of his embodied Spirit.

everyday's a happy birthday
knowing i can find daddy
at the beach.

NEGRÓGEBRA

Black calculus #1

how many faces must i wear to be safe
in the eyes of those without the melanin making us "other?"
do i smile with teeth or will it be mistaken for a sneer?
do i have to walk in the middle of the street whistling dixie
or
can i walk on the same sidewalk asking myself if it's safe?

Black calculus #2

how hard do i have to work to be visible in your systems?
walking into the school system I work "twice as hard" to be noticed
which makes me twice as smart and still invisible
i have to run three times as fast because i was born left behind
at the back of the line because i will always be Black

Black calculus #3

where in world can i be whole when your systems continue
to measure me based on your flaws and standards? i never measure up!
i am always reduced to simplest form like numerators and denominators
divided by a common factor
i am as human as you and yet, your patriarchy tells me,
"do as i say, not as i do!"

Black calculus #4

a tsunami of variables
the nonwhite the non male and the "others"
drowning in servitude feeding the privileged

starving the 'others' barely surviving while not
"others" are thriving.

Black calculus #5

how do you reconcile abundance with a constant of inequity?
why does a wealth of resources never meet the needs of the greedy,
and never, ever meet the needs of the needy?

Black calculus #6

will my silence be mistaken for "talking back!?" will my success
be the reason to change the results? will i be listened to
if i have the wrong accent?
if i show too much passion, will i be misunderstood, again?
if i say, "no!" will that be the reason to take the safety off?
will you be threatened
if i look you in the eye, without fear? or distrust me
because i look away in disgust?

Black calculus #7

do i fill out the profile describing my experience and favorite feature?
or will "a Black man fitting my description..." say all there is to know
about me? how can i claim to be a proud amerikan after i'm told to,
"go back to where you came from!?" do i dare ask, "where's
your birth certificate, pilgrim?"

Black calculus #8

two expressions looking for balance an equation
always in a state of inequalities greater than less than
never equal to...

Black calculus #9

If seven bullets ain't enough to kill a Black man,   how can the excuse,
"i feared for my life"   for murder by uniform,
                                        not be valid?

Black calculus #10

If death by hanging,   and starving a race
by involuntary sterilization   doesn't eliminate the threat
when will the amerikan revolution
                                revolt in my favor?

MIND MAKES LOVE

what we do to love
if we hold on to hope too tight
if we hold on to hugs for too long
if we hold on to dreams
we think they belong to the holder.

if we let threads unravel too easily
if we let perfect get in the way
if we let go of fire
we think the magic is gone forever

what has mind done to love?
mind has made love
unreal
        disguised
                camouflaged
        unseen
and unfelt
yet thought about   enough   to doubt   it exists.

SWEAT TEARS BLOOD

spilling guts where they need to be spread.

blood
sweat
tears of struggle

mopped up like a mess that needs cleaning.

red turning rusty stains.
chalk outlined shapes
thrown overboard

no!
jumping "shackled!"
gifting life, and conscious mind,
for others to live life. for others to harvest dreams!
brick and mortar foundation
ground outta the bones of ancestors.
filling in spaces barely surviving in places.

a precious where hope flourishes.
Spirit sees with vision beyond distance and time.
feel inspiration pounding through your arteries
sweat
burning tears
and blood

thriving beyond expectations.
something to cherish!

A SONG FROM MAMA

music in my bones, sucking on bay leaves
to charm her throat singin' her heart out where she sits
too many stairs up to the choir pulpit choral procession passing her
climbing the too steep stairs grab the hymnal "turn to page..."
  sing along with mama broadway musical
standards set high always ready for a rogers and hammerstein
song and dance routine belting from just beneath her bottom ribs
whipping warm air up through expectant vocal chords
bending vibrations spinning through the hollowed out roof
of her mouth melodic tunes polished into the shape of her voice
rich curving harmonies heart strings vibrating like a cello's baritone
  the fullness of a mature vital life.
  the envy of club grandma!

THE LAKE IN HER CALM

a placid surface
the face of meditation
still smooth flat
unaffected
by the weight of the column of air over the lake

a reflection allowed in the balance a silent OM hums without sound
whispers like inner doubts shushing air before
breezes like mistrusts and distrusts turn into
gale force winds
projections, no matter how false
move the faithful
like waves on the lake
winds blowing foot high waves like waders returning to the beach
the rush of life the echoes of foreign voices
translating their inner disruptions
over a search for balance tell the lake to meditate harder.

MEMORIES OF THE FUTURE

love based in memories   past joys   passions spent
falling in love are not reasons   for staying there.
dreams are memories of the future.
                    now   motivates my next impulse
faith in today's path   leads to tomorrow lessons
                        meeting fears with confidence
fully filling each breath   like blood fills my heart
                        knowing my purpose   is resisting the suffocating
expectations of others.   rising in love   expanding still.

VILLAGE MEDICINE

stories change lives   the village narratives   integrate the world
the self in the world   building selves   sustaining some bodies
the village grows the child
nourishing dreams   that echo   echo   echo
in conscious thought   AND   action
boldly proclaiming   "I CAN..."
while systems say
"you can't...!"

the village harvests   experiences filling the child with enough love
to share forward.
love needs love.
don't do the math...
they'll say
it doesn't add up.

THE TEACHER SPACE

the only adult in the room looking out for their inner
twelve year old special ed student victimized by fear of catching
autism as if it were a "cootie" to catch

looking out for all their misfit friends that weren't allowed
to eat with "normal kids" at the long table in the cafeteria

bullies don't feel safe picking on the teacher's pets
since all of the students feel like the favorite

empathy is the thread woven through patterns of speech
remembering imagined threats of ridicule and disdain
resolved to open windows sealed behind false bravado
fear wearing the rugged individual like a tent with bootstraps
so strong they pull themselves up

victims no longer silent voices found becoming advocates
for what is fair and just in a system weighted in
favor of the privileged, pre-schooled two-parented tradition

the teacher's heart beats the memories of all the feelings
of acceptance and alienation of inclusion winning over exclusion
of rushing from the margins to the center
of our attention.
we are all welcome here!

LOVE HAPPENS

inspiration comes from
overdue overlooked
communication

connections through a variety of capsules
and spin cycles synchronized
to overlap
a three dimensional venn diagram
experiences and perspectives
evolving
spinning
growing forward
dispersing dichotomies.
hearts working to the same beat all chambers full
refilling
never taking for the sake of taking
always giving forgiving.

LOVE MISSING...

my heart aches for all the first times i saw your face
the beats that were skipped the joys washing over me
fears of missing out hanging in my shame closet
holding on with enough heart to live another lifetime
how many breaths taken away hoping for the weight of your gaze
to fall on me stronger than gravity stealing oxygen and light
unlike a black hole your horizon is up front arms reaching around me
like an equator filling my life and time your presence.

LOOKING FOR BALANCE

i want for you what you want for me there should be an
equal sign between us. coming to an understanding is a
multi-step equation i listen to you you listen to me
i talk to you you talk to me
you "feel" me i "feel" you
is that true for you? not for me
let's listen, talk and "feel" some more.
we "add" hope to both sides
we "take away" fear from both sides
sometimes
we may need to "divide" our resources that we have enough to share
imagine the possibilities "multiplied" when we work together
finding the truth of understanding is
NOT the truth in you NOT the truth in me
BUT
the truth between us like an equal sign.

AN EQUAL SIGN

life is an algebraic expression   looking for equilibrium.
variables and constants accounted for   variables shift spontaneously
beyond the speed of calculation   constants   shifting
is where life gets tricky.
        what you said yesterday   was
your word   immutable…   and yet,
        attached to a thought   no longer unchanged
new additions   multiplied   since yesterday.
            attention divided   by the past
with an eye   on the future
now   the constant's constant.
        no need to search out more variables
between the waves   disappearing beneath the surf
            the fullness of now   has enough unknowns
in the oncoming horizon,
observing with detachment   lets the present unwrap,
until the moment of inertia,   achieving an inevitable conclusion
now
        embedded in my DNA,   interacting with   detachment
participating in   now
        without holding onto it.

so much for equilibrium.

A SENSE OF PLACE

a new dawn
on a celestial body
where everyone flies.
double waxing
crescent moans
float just below the horizon.
warm breezes gasp gently
over dark bronzing
flesh-toned peaks kissed by
haloed clouds
prickly hearts shiver than
melt over subterranean fires.
i am not a stranger
in this place.

LULLABY WAVES

listening to silence space between hugs
time between synchronized heart beats
i can watch dreams change around the edges clouds
changing like tides unseen turbulence still!
silence deafening dampening hope with falling rain tears
steam not smoke rising out of smoldering embers no sound
no vibe no distance to close stay safe in sound
there's enough silence between heart beats if you're listening
for love.

WHAT YOU SAW

how i feel   shows up on my face,   a quarter of a smile
a glint of light shining out of my eyes   a listening stare
into middle space
a straight line of lips   where luscious lives   eyebrows throwing shade
my feelings come   from a wordless place...   i can't explain!
doesn't mean   "i don't know!"
the fog of whim   a cross breeze   a silent pause
in my mind   logic is not enough
i must "be"   with my feelings   an "inneraction"
that creates a dialogue   with the muse
at last   words   resounding with   curious probes
nuanced ambiguities   mean nothing
mean everything   though,   all they heard was,
a shrug of the shoulders saying   "i don't know!"

RECIPROCAL TO LOVE

unconditional love
has no "quid pro quo"
no "tit for tat"
no this for that
not heavy   but rooted in the marrow   of our bone cells
invent love as you go?
how does a river   build its banks,   looking for borders
to flow inside of?

love given freely
love,   reciprocal to love
yields   unyielding love   overflowing
never runs out...   never!   love demands
always   met   because love is   no demands
love is   all   ways   ready!

natural as   breathing in   fingertips tingling
breathing   out   no waiting to exhale
love   pouring outta pores   open to all
in the circle   overlapping circles   surrounded by more circles
hearts beating in   synchrony
feels like a
symphony
definitely
synergy
when every   one feels it like
gravity,
drawn to
unconditional love.

DON'T SPARE ME!

you walk barefoot close to your edges. razor blades
gang planks and cliffs
the abyss calls your name inviting the flight of life
offering a falling
death
a two way mirror fogged by pipe dream martyrdom looking at the
place that would swallow your drowning footsteps whole
leaving no trace of ever being present
a never existence a black hole
not even a witness to your absence
not even a memory to be forgotten
why bother taking the next breath unless
it is filled with fire? passion for sharing the experience
of healing wounds caused by loving too much.
go there...! love healing is
regenerating
recreating
reincarnating
rebirthing
‘ reborning’ anew.
unknown to thy self. a gift of purpose!

STOP!

i'm doing my best   to just stand there
          and don't move!
                                        the only thing   i'm resisting
is gravity,
          so i can just stand   here   and don't move!
if i fall over   and don't move   at the same time
am i going to be resisting...?
if it's gravity,
                    will i need wings to fly?   if it's an arrest,
gravity   will win

over my dead body!

NO BETTER TIME

the present is NOW! not the now of before or after.
not the now of yesterday or tomorrow.
do not be lulled to sleep believing there will be a day after today.
do not get caught up in the memories of the day before yesterday.
procrastinating on living NOW,
hoping for better conditions to live happily ever after. putting
living on hold, rubbing hands together warming the globe,
against record cold, glaciers melting while oceans rise,
changing geography islands blown off the map. dams breaking,
floods of hate causing fires to burn like revenge
for the drought El Niño y La Niña ocean currents,
like mischievous children looking for shrinking tropical forests,
where fresh water used to be
recycled,
refreshed
replenished,
there to be enough for all of us. NOW is the rainy day
we've been saving for imagine human error being the wake up call
that puts us all to sleep. imagine the one human's error
being the off switch to an enlightened vision of tomorrow.
raise the words outta the throats of our legacy. we are the ones
we have been waiting for!
ancestors, dreaming for centuries have conjured us
to be here
NOW! their dream is not for us to be suffering,
voiceless, no authority over our lives. we are expected to bring
the brilliance of our collective vision, to bear on the darkness
ignorance has wrought. a rude awakening for many realizing how
the power of love and non-violence will be a new kind of trauma
breaking the heart of hate you know, "the revolution
will not be televised" because the media will not shine a camera on

a heart that is healing, not bleeding,
sharing true love,
fiercely.

A SENSE LESS HEART

the only way to "know" my feelings is to "feel" my feelings
moving forward in my path there is no distance between here
and there changing the "organ" of impulses and feelings
has to be a "fall" from the restrictions and mandates from the mind
in the brain "down" to a heart beating, throbbing, pulsing,
feeling love is an endless flight into the depths of light.
wings open to catch weightless senses awake alive
with self awareness without knowledge because the mind
would have you believe there is a sequence of words a description
with a period at the end of it for feelings that change
like breezes flowing between molecules of love
no name no direction to go come from
what is the distance between thoughts and feelings?
we prioritize challenges by being a human thinking,
thinking feelings just don't make sense.
...senseless

AMBIVALENCE

the irony is that gaia will continue to be bella
whether we see her or not!
whether we are moved to tears,
or not!

she is ambivalent to her beauty and glory, while we are humbled
by her presence aún su ausέncia

she will still bless flowers with their scent
whether our noses catch a whiff on the wind,
or
notice the breeze with a hint of...
'¿qué sé yo?'

she will share her blues with the sky from the darkest
midnight blue to the blue that is translucent
like the nearly, still waters at the end of a wave.

the miracle, that we notice that we are allowed
to witness gaiamundo in all her minute
esplendor, is the blessing

the solitude of this quarantine has inspired visions
of how it could be if we got out
of our own way.

WHAT YOU WON'T DO

islands are lonely
they're afraid of the water
because they don't know how to swim
waiting on a ferry better build a bridge.
fill the ocean with lava wait for the seas to dry up
learn to love alone

INNERVERSE

dreams are   like the
scenes   drawn across galaxies
like the,   constellations   posing in space   like the
            archetypes   described in mythology
across generations of humanity.
when i close my eyes   it is not   blocking out light
            making me believe dark.
my inner vision   behind closed eyelids,
sees light a different way.   all perceptions
                are distorted realities   when seen
from different perspectives.
i'm in trouble   ignoring others' perceptions   as possibilities of reality
in my innerverse.   though red horizons
portend toxic atmospheres   like dusk transforms
day to night   outer light
filtered through closed eyelids   shines brilliance   flowing away like
sheets   billowing in my heart's   exhalation of love.   closed
eyelids   transform me from   what you perceive   to my natural
state   stardust!   awake   to both the universe
we share   and my innerverse   a shaky balance
                                     between nows.

COME TRUE DREAMS

the melancholy in the doorway between times coming and going
the power of now the intensity of all my inputs
on the instant in front of me belies the dream i am planting
in an open heart any open mind a future
that is brilliant when we share love with the one
next to the "other" one.
harvesting flaming arrows sparks of dreams launched into the future
a blaze of hope and consciousness a realization come true
meteors flying off rough hewn diamonds hearts dedicated
to the unmet needs brought to class minds invested
in learning like oxygen surrounding a glowing ember
one more spark explodes into a firestorm.
fighting fires started intentionally burning down myths
that a grade defines the learning that asking questions
means you don't know that knowing answers
makes anyone smarter.

HEART BREAKING LOVE

i'm supposed to be   done with you
heart shattered   epic fall out of love
          no parachute   crashed landings on
islands in the abyss   lifesavers   only hard candy circles
drifting out of reach   overwhelming inertia   evolving me
into a black hole   no good life survives life
i must be my own gravity   even if i can only attract light
moments are lived to thrive in.   stretching expectations
expanding dreams
have no end   love and hope,   light and direction   power me
across my innerverse   a changing current   in the love stream
does not flow back on itself   moving away   from   now
          will always be   forward.

HEAD OVER HEELS

submerged in air down to the soles of my feet
didn't know breathing all this time has been
holding my breath all my life waiting
to inhale mother earth without fear of drowning
underground planted like primordial seeds all we need
is in the earth not fallow but dormant over millennia
waiting for a breach in the womb for the light
of love to breathe forth a germination of Spirit

THE SAME HORIZON

one water   one coast
interrupted only   by man-made canals
we are watching the same wave   arriving always,
with that crushing   churning whisper   the rhythmic white noise
of dying waves
how many winds blow between us?
fog blurring our vision   are we still standing   on the same earth,
connected by our humanity,   one race of human beings?
it is we   that create   the unbridged moats
crevasses   canyons   the distances
sweeping away from us.
          it is one brilliant sun   we watch melting
into a red pool,   pouring out of the sky
into the same horizon.

BALLAST IN THE FLOW

what we choose to weigh us down grief
a dam overflowing with tears the ease and flight

of falling in love the work it takes to stay there memories of being
overjoyed remembering only the good parts obsessions that spin
like eddies looking for a bottom to get to the weight of promises
broken never kept the gravity
of aborted happily ever afters
what we hold onto for dear life keeps us from capsizing
drifting into a weightless vacuum, alone.

SACRED SECRET

love is so sacred it becomes a secret
we dare not show we dare not tell
a sign of weakness a show of strength
to say you feel it too strong too soon
never too much
unimagined undeserved unrequited
unaccepted rejected, three times
unreciprocated unspoken
never tell don't want them to know afraid ashamed
that it's unreasonable unbelievable like it can't be true
i love you takes faith makes a promise keeps a
promise fingers crossed behind my back thinking
there's a way out an escape dig a basement
a back door to doubt love
am i worth it?

WRITTEN IN LIFE

walking outta the corner of my eye through a puddle of tears
circles of sadness spread out from each step
melancholy clings like honey around my feet marking my path
like bread crumbs through a field of mourn winds of time
blow in all directions mourn knows where to find me
in currents pulsing a chamber full of closets
marked only by a crease in time
where ancestors remember and remiss
memories of lives too many to count.
lives lived like a map
guiding me to places destinies not destinations
visions to fulfill written in the winds
beneath my feet!

WHERE I LIVE

my home is   the land   of humanity.
love,   with its vibration,   deserves,   even the possibility,
of connecting us   like reasons
                                        like rhymes
                                                            like rhythms,
                                        like tones,
                    like the music
that has colors
                that have steps to a dance   with at least one,
other human being!
love like blood   saves all of us   by sharing each,   both,
       severally and jointly   love and blood.

CLASSROOM GUIDE

LOVE

Love is more than an emotion that is shared between individuals. Love is more than a feeling acted out on another being. It is something that we strive to attain in our relationships because it is satisfying and fulfilling, and it feels good! Love is so much more than the words used to describe it.

- Describe your definition of love
- How does the dictionary define love?
- How does your definition compare to the dictionary definition?

In the poem, "love missing," the word "love" only appears in the title. Is there love in this poem?

- Where is the love situated?
- Is it in the poet?
- Is it in the reader?
- Is the love in another person?
- Is the love in this poem make believe?

Be prepared to share your thinking about any of these questions.

The following poems do not use the word "love" in the context of the poem:

"Written in Life"
"At the Beach"
"Ballast in the Flow"

- What notions of love does the poet allude to in each of these pieces?

- Describe how love and melancholy are connected?
- How is mourning an expression of love?
- Where is the love?

Review the following poems:

"Sacred Secret"
"Mind Makes Love"

- How does society use love as collateral?
- Do we "think" about love for how it "feels" or for how it makes us "feel"?
- Is love a space created between the giver and the receiver?

Read one of the poems aloud to a(n) partner/audience:

"Head Over Heels"
"the lake in her calm"
"Sweat, Tears, and Blood"

Discuss the type of love that shows up in the selected poem, as compared to the dictionary definition. Choose another one of the poems and repeat the prompt.

MATHEMATICS

Read the following poems:

"Looking for Balance,"
"Reciprocal to Love"
"an equal sign"

- What elements of mathematics are embedded in these pieces?
  - How do those elements of mathematics support the flow of

love between two entities?

- How would a mathematician feel about mathematics being used as a vehicle to convey love?
- Which words, interaction or transaction, best describe the emotional exchange in these poems?
- Does love require a mutual effort by the participants?

In the poem "negrogebra" there is mathematical vocabulary.

- Describe which mathematics words are used in their traditional contexts.
- Describe which words, used in mathematical contexts, surprised you in this poem.
- What other contexts are mixed in with the mathematics in the poem?
- How does the poet highlight privilege in the poem?
  - Who has the privilege? What's your evidence?
- Does the "voice" in this poem speak from the perspective of the protagonist or the antagonist? What evidence do you "hear" to support your thinking?

In the poem, "where i live," how does love manifest as a place?

SOCIETY

Read aloud the following poems:

"STOP!"
"negrógebra"
"No better time"

Discuss within a homogenous (gender and/or ethnicity) affinity group:

- what are the hazards of being in the skin you're in?
- how can you view the events described in the selected poems through the lens of privilege?

ACKNOWLEDGEMENTS

I want to recognize my family's support for moving me forward in the publishing of this collection of poems. My daughters, Lucia and Ava, encourage me to write whenever I can. My mother, Gloria, is one of my biggest fans, because she likes that my poetry makes her think.

I want to thank my friends, students, and colleagues for believing in me. They imagine that I can make a difference in the world by sharing what I think, what I feel and what I write about this life endeavor.

I am grateful to my compoetas in the poetry community for recognizing my voice in the written word and for encouraging me to "speak my piece" into an open mic whenever one is available.

I would like to appreciate the hosts, curators, and presenters that open up space for me and all the brave poets that share their stories, in all the venues and virtual spaces that document "our story."

Finally, I am grateful to Tongo Eisen-Martin for bringing his poetic and musical insights to bear on the "voice," calling out from in front of and behind the words on the page. Thank you, J. K. Fowler, publisher of Nomadic Press for supporting this project, sharing resources that helped bring forward a product I am proud of.

Many thanks to the following publications, where a few of the pieces have previously appeared:

"Innerverse," *The City is Already Speaking: Poetry from San Francisco Bookstore Readings* (Volume 2)

"Ambivalence," *Poetry in The Time of Coronavirus* (Volume Two)

NORM MATTOX

is a native New Yorker, returning to New York after raising a family in the San Francisco Bay Area for over 30 years. Norm recently retired from the San Francisco Unified School District after 27 years as a bilingual educator. Norm is a teacher for life so the next modality of teaching and learning will be through poetry that tells a story of love in a time of challenge and struggle.

Norm has shared his poetry as a featured reader around the San Francisco Bay Area, as well as in the global zoom arena.

NOMADIC PRESS
BLACK WRITERS FUND

NOMADIC PRESS
EMERGENCY FUND

OTHER WAYS TO SUPPORT NOMADIC PRESS' WRITERS

In 2020, two funds geared specifically toward supporting our writers were created: the **Nomadic Press Black Writers Fund** and the **Nomadic Press Emergency Fund**.

The former is a forever fund that puts money directly into the pockets of our Black writers. The latter provides up to $200 dignity-centered emergency grants to any of our writers in need.

Please consider supporting these funds. You can also more generally support Nomadic Press by donating to our general fund via nomadicpress.org/donate and by continuing to buy our books. As always, thank you for your support!

Scan here for more information and/or to donate.
You can also donate at nomadicpress.org/store.